QUOTES
on WRITING

by WRITERS for WRITERS

650
quotes to inspire, encourage and amuse writers

Compiled by Kevin Berry

The copyright for each individual quote belongs to the person who said it. The arrangement of the quotes into these sections is my own.

ISBN-13: 978-1536902891
ISBN-10: 1536902896

Dragonflight Publishing

My website:
kevinberrybooks.com

Cover design:
Amanda Sinclair
Radiate Design
Radiatedesign.co.nz

This book uses UK spelling and punctuation conventions.

CONTENTS

INTRODUCTION

These 650 quotes are a source of inspiration and encouragement to me as a writer when my own words are not flowing, when I feel isolated as a result of my chosen vocation, or merely when I want to smile at the wit and wisdom of renowned authors.

I've compiled the quotes into a short reference book in the hope that other writers will derive the same benefit and enjoyment from them that I do. The quotes are organised into sections. This categorisation is my own. You may disagree with how I've arranged some of them; some quotes would probably fit two or more categories, and I put them where I thought they most belonged.

Why writers write is the first section. Then we progress to how writers plan their writing (or not) and their thoughts on the infamous condition of writer's block. Many quotes follow on the actual physical process of writing, how to make your prose sing, and on editing and revising your early drafts.

There are sections in which the quotes cover various attributes of writers that you might identify with at different times: the persistent, the prolific, the passionate, the private, the perfectionist and even the pernicious.

Sections follow on the pain, and pleasure, of writing, then a large section on philosophical quotes that I didn't feel were obvious candidates for any other category. The penultimate section is on puns, parodies and other funny stuff.

The final section contains the most potent quotes I've found. I come back to those again and again and never tire of reading them. If you only read one chapter of this book, make it this one.

Enjoy!

And, if you come across any particularly good quotes and would like to send them to me, I'd be happy to include them in an updated version of this book. Be sure to let me know who said any quote you send.

THE PURPOSE OF WRITING

The purpose of a writer is to keep civilization from destroying itself.
> — *Albert Camus*

One writes to make a home for oneself, on paper, in time and in others' minds.
> — *Alfred Kazin*

The writer writes in order to teach himself, to understand himself, to satisfy himself; the publishing of his ideas, though it brings gratification, is a curious anti-climax.
> — *Alfred Kazin*

I believe one writes because one has to create a world in which one can live.
> — *Anaïs Nin*

The role of a writer is not to say what we all can say, but what we are unable to say.
> — *Anaïs Nin*

We write to taste life twice, in the moment and in retrospect.
        — Anaïs Nin

I am aware of being in a beautiful prison, from which I can only escape by writing.
        — Anaïs Nin

I want to write, but more than that, I want to bring out all kinds of things that lie buried deep in my heart.
        — Anne Frank

Writing and reading decrease our sense of isolation. They deepen and widen and expand our sense of life: they feed the soul.
        — Anne Lamott

You write to communicate to the hearts and minds of others what's burning inside you. And we edit to let the fire show through the smoke.
        — Arthur Plotnik

A story is a letter that the author writes to himself, to tell himself things that he would be unable to discover otherwise.
        — Carlos Ruiz Zafón

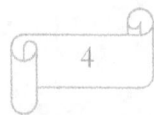

I write because I cannot *not* write.
— *Charlotte Brontë*

Good fiction's job is to comfort the disturbed and disturb the comfortable.
— *David Wallace*

All that I hope to say in books, all that I ever hope to say, is that I love the world.
— *E B White*

All a writer wants is to be read, and people are so flattering and lovely. I mean, there are witches out there as well. But most are so kind.
— *E L James*

I write to understand as much as to be understood.
— *Elie Wiesel*

For a true writer, each book should be a new beginning where he tries again for something that is beyond attainment. He should always try for something that has never been done or that others have tried and failed. Then sometimes, with great luck, he will succeed.
— *Ernest Hemingway*

I write because I don't know what I think until I read what I say.
> — *Flannery O'Connor*

Fairy tales do not tell children that dragons exist. Children already know that dragons exist. Fairy tales tell children the dragons can be killed.
> — *G K Chesterton*

When I sit down to write a book, I do not say to myself, "I am going to produce a work of art." I write it because there is some lie that I want to expose, some fact to which I want to draw attention, and my initial concern is to get a hearing.
> — *George Orwell*

Any writer worth his salt writes to please himself … It's a self-exploratory operation that is endless. An exorcism of not necessarily his demon, but of his divine discontent.
> — *Harper Lee*

I write for the same reason I breathe … because if I didn't, I would die.
> — *Isaac Asimov*

I only know that in a subtle way or in a hidden way, I want to have an impact on the reader's heart and mind.
> — *Isabel Allende*

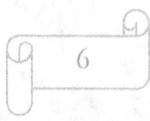

I'm a writer, and I will write what I want to write.
— *J K Rowling*

I don't really write with an audience in mind. I write for myself and hope someone else likes to read it.
— *Jillian Medoff*

I write entirely to find out what I'm thinking, what I'm looking at, what I see and what it means. What I want and what I fear.
— *Joan Didion*

The novelist's job is to see and say clearly what people are.
— *John Masters*

Never tell a story because it is true: tell it because it is a good story.
— *John Pentland Mahaffy*

I want to write books that unlock the traffic jam in everybody's head.
— *John Updike*

Why do I write? It's not that I want people to think I am smart, or even that I'm a good writer. I write because I want to end my loneliness.
— *Jonathan Safran Foer*

I write to give myself strength. I write to be the characters that I am not. I write to explore all the things I'm afraid of.
— *Joss Whedon*

We all love storytelling, and as a writer you get to tell stories all the time.
— *Joyce Carol Oates*

The writer must earn money in order to be able to live and to write, but he must by no means live and write for the purpose of making money.
— *Karl Marx*

I just wrote because it was fun.
— *Kasey Michaels*

If you can't annoy somebody, there is little point in writing.
— *Kingsley Amis*

A bird doesn't sing because it has an answer, it sings because it has a song.
— *Maya Angelou*

Writing isn't generally a lucrative source of income; only a few, exceptional writers reach the income levels associated with the best-sellers. Rather, most of us write because we can make a modest living, or even supplement our day jobs, doing something about which we feel passionately. Even at the worst of times, when nothing goes right, when the prose is clumsy and the ideas feel stale, at least we're doing something that we genuinely love. There's no other reason to work this hard, except that love.
— *Melissa Scott*

Why does one begin to write? Because she feels misunderstood, I guess. Because it never comes out clearly enough when she tries to speak. Because she wants to rephrase the world, to take it in and give it back again differently, so that everything is used and nothing is lost. Because it's something to do to pass the time until she is old enough to experience the things she writes about.
— *Nicole Krauss*

That is why I write — to try to turn sadness into longing, solitude into remembrance.
— *Paulo Coelho*

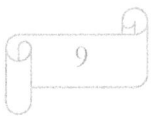

I think every fiction writer, to a certain extent, is a schizophrenic and able to have two or three or five voices in his or her body. We seek, through our profession, to get those voices onto paper.
— *Ridley Pearson*

A person is a fool to become a writer. His only compensation is absolute freedom. He has no master except his own soul, and that, I am sure, is why he does it.
— *Roald Dahl*

No man but a blockhead ever wrote, except for money.
— *Samuel Johnson*

Write the book you most long to read.
— *Steven Saylor*

The goal, I suppose, any fiction writer has, no matter what your subject, is to hit the human heart and the tear ducts and the nape of the neck and to make a person feel something about what the characters are going through and to experience the moral paradoxes and struggles of being human.
— *Tim O'Brien*

One of the things that draws writers to writing is that they can get things right that they got wrong in real life.
　　　　　— *Tobias Wolff*

So long as you write what you wish to write, that is all that matters; and whether it matters for ages or only for hours, nobody can say.
　　　　　— *Virginia Woolf*

We do not write because we want to; we write because we have to.
　　　　　— *W Somerset Maugham*

Writing is my way of expressing — and thereby eliminating — all the various ways we can be wrong-headed.
　　　　　— *Zadie Smith*

THE PANTSER

I'm not the sort of writer who can plan out things. Mostly I have no idea where I'm going.
— *Chang-Rae Lee*

Don't rush or force the ending of a story or book. All you have to know is the next scene.
— *Chuck Palahniuk*

Writing a novel is like driving a car at night. You can only see as far as your headlights, but you can make the whole trip that way.
— *E. L. Doctorow*

First, find out what your hero wants. Then just follow him.
— *Ray Bradbury*

When in doubt, have a man come through the door with a gun in his hand.
— *Raymond Chandler*

Occasionally, there arises a writing situation where you see an alternative to what you are doing, a mad, wild gamble of a way for handling something, which may leave you looking stupid, ridiculous or brilliant — you just don't know which. You can play it safe there, too, and proceed along the route you'd mapped out for yourself. Or you can trust your personal demon who delivered that crazy idea in the first place.

Trust your demon.

— *Roger Zelazny*

If you haven't got an idea, start a story anyway. You can always throw it away, and maybe by the time you get to the fourth page you *will* have an idea, and you'll only have to throw away the first three pages.

— *William Campbell Gault*

THE PLOTTER

The best time for planning a book is while you're doing the dishes.
— *Agatha Christie*

You can't lose if you give them handsome highwaymen, duels, three-foot fountains and whacking great horses and dogs all over the place.
— *Barbara Cartland*

Writing a novel is like heading out over the open sea in a small boat. It helps if you have a plan and a course laid out.
— *John Gardner*

In writing a series of stories about the same characters, plan the whole series in advance in some detail, to avoid contradictions and inconsistencies.
— *L Sprague de Camp*

You don't actually have to write anything until you've thought it out. This is an enormous relief, and you can sit there searching for the point at which the story becomes a toboggan and starts to slide.
— *Marie de Nervaud*

I keep an elaborate calendar for my characters detailing on which dates everything happens. I'm constantly revising this as I go along. It gives me the freedom to intricately plot my story, knowing it will at least hold up on a timeline.
— *Maria Semple*

If you do enough planning before you start to write, there's no way you can have writer's block. I do a complete chapter by chapter outline.
— *R L Stine*

THE PROCRASTINATOR, AND OVERCOMING WRITER'S BLOCK

The secret of getting ahead is getting started.
— *Agatha Christie*

The thing all writers do best is find ways to avoid writing.
— *Alan Dean Foster*

I'm not patient at all. I avoid writer's block by writing. I power through with a bad version, so I can move on, and usually once I've gotten to the next scene, I'll discover what was missing from the bad version scene. Then I can easily rewrite it to get back on the right path.
— *Anders Holm*

People have writer's block not because they can't write, but because they despair of writing eloquently.
— *Anna Quindlen*

Writers write while dreamers procrastinate.
— *Besa Kosova*

Cats are dangerous companions for writers because cat watching is a near-perfect method of writing avoidance.
— *Dan Greenburg*

If you wait for inspiration to write, you're not a writer, you're a waiter.
— *Dan Poynter*

Nothing's a better cure for writer's block than to eat ice cream right out of the carton.
— *Don Roff*

Planning to write is not writing. Outlining, researching, talking to people about what you're doing, none of that is writing. Writing is writing.
— *E L Doctorow*

I don't believe in writer's block or waiting for inspiration. If you're a writer, you sit down and write.
— *Elmore Leonard*

If you wish to be a writer, write.
— *Epictetus*

I went for years not finishing anything. Because, of course, when you finish something you can be judged.
— *Erica Jong*

The hard part about writing a novel is finishing it.
— *Ernest Hemingway*

Perhaps it would be better not to be a writer, but if you must, then write. If all feels hopeless, if that famous "inspiration" will not come, write. If you are a genius, you'll make your own rules, but if not - and the odds are against it — go to your desk no matter what your mood, face the icy challenge of the paper — write.
— *J B Priestley*

I've often said that there's no such thing as writer's block; the problem is idea block.
— *Jeffrey Deaver*

My cure for writer's block is to step away from the thing I'm stuck on, usually a novel, and write something totally different.
— *Jess Walter*

You can't think yourself out of a writing block; you have to write yourself out of a thinking block.
— *John Rogers*

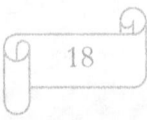

Every writer I know has trouble writing.
— *Joseph Heller*

I always do the first line well, but I have trouble doing the others.
— *Moliere*

Being a writer is a very peculiar sort of a job: it's always you versus a blank sheet of paper (or a blank screen) and quite often the blank piece of paper wins.
— *Neil Gaiman*

Being a real writer means being able to do the work on a bad day.
— *Norman Mailer*

I just sit at my typewriter and curse a bit.
— *P G Wodehouse*

As a writer, I need an enormous amount of time alone. Writing is 90 percent procrastination: reading magazines, eating cereal out of the box, watching infomercials. It's a matter of doing everything you can to avoid writing, until it is about four in the morning and you reach the point where you have to write. Having anybody watching that or attempting to share it with me would be grisly.
— *Paul Rudnik*

Don't wait for moods. You accomplish nothing if you do that. Your mind must know it has got to get down to work.
— *Pearl S Buck*

One reason I don't suffer writer's block is that I don't wait on the muse, I summon it at need.
— *Piers Anthony*

Inspiration is a guest that does not willingly visit the lazy.
— *Pyotr Tchaikovsky*

I get a lot of letters from people. They say: "I want to be a writer. What should I do?" I tell them to stop writing to me and get on with it.
— *Ruth Rendell*

Everything in life is writable about if you have the outgoing guts to do it, and the imagination to improvise. The worst enemy to creativity is self-doubt.
— *Sylvia Plath*

If I'm trying to sleep, the ideas won't stop. If I'm trying to write, there appears a barren nothingness.
— *Terri Guillemets*

The only cure for writer's block is insomnia.
— *Terri Guillemets*

Writer's block is a disease for which there is no cure, only respite.
— *Terri Guillemets*

A writer is somebody for whom writing is more difficult than it is for other people.
— *Thomas Mann*

Wait, wait, wait, wait. Don't try to write through it, to force it. Many do, but that won't work. Just wait, it will come.
— *Toni Morrison*

Don't be a writer; be writing.
— *William Faulkner*

The easiest thing to do on earth is not write.
— *William Goldman*

THE PROCESS OF WRITING

I've always believed in writing without a collaborator, because when two people are writing the same book, each believes he gets all the worries and only half the royalties.
— *Agatha Christie*

There was a moment when I changed from an amateur to a professional. I assumed the burden of a profession, which is to write even when you don't want to, don't much like what you're writing, and aren't writing particularly well.
— *Agatha Christie*

True ease in writing comes from art, not chance, as those who move easiest have learned to dance.
— *Alexander Pope*

To know is nothing at all; to imagine is everything.
— *Anatole France*

Writing is a job, a talent, but it's also the place to go in your head. It is the imaginary friend you drink your tea with in the afternoon.
— *Ann Patchett*

If you want to be a writer, write. Write and write and write. If you stop, start again. Save everything that you write. If you feel blocked, write through it until you feel your creative juices flowing again. Write. Writing is what makes a writer, nothing more and nothing less.
— *Anne Rice*

The one ironclad rule is that I have to try. I have to walk into my writing room and pick up my pen every weekday morning.
— *Anne Tyler*

My own experience is that once a story has been written, one has to cross out the beginning and the end. It is there that we authors do most of our lying.
— *Anton Chekhov*

A catless writer is almost inconceivable; even Ernest Hemingway, manly follower of the hunting trophy and the bullfight, lived waist-deep in cats. It's a perverse taste, really, since it would be easier to write with a herd of buffalo in the room than even one cat; they make nests in the notes and bite the end of the pen and walk on the typewriter keys.
— *Barbara Holland*

Writing requires the concentration of the writer, demands that nothing else be done except that.
— *Carlos Fuentes*

Writers have two main problems. One is writer's block, when the words won't come at all, and the other is logorrhoea, when the words come so fast that they can hardly get to the wastebasket in time.
— *Cecelia Bartholomeo*

The longer you can allow a story to take shape, the better that final shape will be.
— *Chuck Palahniuk*

I get up in the morning, torture a typewriter until it screams, then stop.
— *Clarence Budington Kelland*

I often will write a scene from three different points of view to find out which has the most tension and which way I'm able to conceal the information I'm trying to conceal. And that is, at the end of the day, what writing suspense is all about.
— *Dan Brown*

The whole trick is to make it feel like you're spying on real people's lives as they get through the day. When I'm writing, I have to trick myself as a writer. If I consciously say, "I'm writing", I feel all this pressure and somehow it doesn't feel as real as when it doesn't seem to count as much.

— *David O Russell*

Writing is an exploration. You start from nothing and learn as you go.

— *E L Doctorow*

The ideal view for daily writing, hour for hour, is the blank brick wall of a cold-storage warehouse. Failing this, a stretch of sky will do, cloudless if possible.

— *Edna Ferber*

All you have to do is write one true sentence. Write the truest sentence that you know.

— *Ernest Hemingway*

There is no rule on how to write. Sometimes it comes easily and perfectly; sometimes it's like drilling rock and then blasting it out with charges.

— *Ernest Hemingway*

You can write any time people will leave you alone and not interrupt you. Or, rather, you can if you will be ruthless enough about it. But the best writing is certainly when you are in love.
— *Ernest Hemingway*

There is no real ending. It's just the place where you stop the story.
— *Frank Herbert*

All I need is a sheet of paper and something to write with, and then I can turn the world upside down.
— *Friedrich Nietzsche*

To write is to write is to write is to write is to write is to write is to write is to write.
— *Gertrude Stein*

Write something, even if it's just a suicide note.
— *Gore Vidal*

Writing, to me, is simply thinking through my fingers.
— *Isaac Asimov*

The wastebasket is the writer's best friend.
— *Isaac Bashevis Singer*

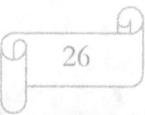

Writing is like making love. Don't worry about the orgasm, just concentrate on the process.
— *Isabel Allende*

I write by hand, making many, many corrections. I would say I cross out more than I write. I have to hunt for words when I speak, and I have the same difficulty when writing.
— *Italo Calvino*

As regards plot I find real life no help at all. Real life seems to have no plots. And as I think a plot desirable and almost necessary, I have this extra grudge against life.
— *Ivy Compton-Burnett*

Writing and cafes are strongly linked in my brain.
— *J K Rowling*

Be ruthless about protecting writing days. Do not cave in to endless requests to have "essential" and "long overdue" meetings on those days.
— *J K Rowling*

One day I will find the right words, and they will be simple.
— *Jack Kerouac*

You write that first draft really to see how it's going to come out.
— *James A Michener*

Don't get it right, just get it written.
— *James Thurber*

Exercise the writing muscle every day, even if it is only a letter, notes, a title list, a character sketch, a journal entry. Writers are like dancers, like athletes. Without that exercise, the muscles seize up.
— *Jane Yolen*

Talent is helpful in writing, but guts are absolutely necessary.
— *Jessamyn West*

Say all you have to say in the fewest possible words, or your reader will be sure to skip them; and in the plainest possible words or he will certainly misunderstand them.
— *John Ruskin*

Write freely and as rapidly as possible and throw the whole thing on paper. Never correct or rewrite until the whole thing is down.
— *John Steinbeck*

Rewrite in process ... interferes with flow and rhythm which come from a kind of unconscious association with the material.
— *John Steinbeck*

Ideas are like rabbits. You get a couple and learn how to handle them, and pretty soon you have a dozen.
— *John Steinbeck*

Abandon the idea that you are ever going to finish. Lose track of the 400 pages and write just one page a day, it helps. Then when it gets finished, you are always surprised.
— *John Steinbeck*

It's doubtful that anyone with an internet connection at his workplace is writing good fiction.
— *Jonathan Franzen*

I was always an early-morning or late-night writer. Early morning was my favourite; late night was because you had a deadline. And at four in the morning, you make up some of your most absurd jokes.
— *Joss Whedon*

The first sentence can't be written until the final sentence is written.
— *Joyce Carol Oates*

Novels begin not on the page, but in meditation and daydreaming — in thinking, not writing.
— *Joyce Carol Oates*

Be daring, take on anything. Don't labour over little cameo works in which every word is to be perfect. Technique holds a reader from sentence to sentence, but only content will stay in his mind.
— *Joyce Carol Oates*

Art is not about thinking something up. It is the opposite — getting something down.
— *Julia Cameron*

Start as close to the end as possible.
— *Kurt Vonnegut*

You learn by writing short stories. Keep writing short stories. The money's in novels, but writing short stories keeps your writing lean and pointed.
— *Larry Niven*

One thing that helps is to give myself permission to write badly. I tell myself that I'm going to do my five or ten pages no matter what, and that I can always tear them up the following morning if I want. I'll have lost nothing — writing and tearing up five pages would leave me no further behind than if I took the day off.
— *Lawrence Block*

Inspiration is wonderful when it happens, but the writer must develop an approach for the rest of the time.
— *Leonard Bernstein*

I must write now and quickly, before I begin to prefer the perfect version that lives in my head.
— *Lettie Prell*

Don't take anyone's writing advice too seriously.
— *Lev Grossman*

Nothing you write, if you hope to be good, will ever come out as you first hoped.
— *Lillian Hellman*

There will come a time when you believe everything is finished; that will be the beginning.
— *Louis L'Amour*

Start writing, no matter what. The water does not flow until the faucet is turned on.
— *Louis L'Amour*

What it takes is to actually write: not to think about it, not to imagine it, not to talk about it, but to actually want to sit down and write.
— *Luanne Rice*

The point of good writing is knowing when to stop.
— *Lucy Montgomery*

A word after a word after a word is power.
— *Margaret Atwood*

Sometimes I wonder if I'm a character being written, or if I'm writing myself.
— *Marilyn Manson*

Write without pay until somebody offers to pay.
— *Mark Twain*

Writing is easy. All you have to do is cross out the wrong words.
— *Mark Twain*

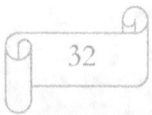

The art of writing is the art of applying the seat of the pants to the seat of the chair.
— *Mary Heaton Vorse*

Get it down. Bumble it through. Tell the story. When you have fifty or a hundred pages typed, you've got something to work with.
— *Mary Higgins Clark*

There are those critics — New York critics as a rule — who say, "Well, Maya Angelou has a new book out and of course it's good but then she's a natural writer." Those are the ones I want to grab by the throat and wrestle to the floor because it takes me forever to get it to sing. I work at the language.
— *Maya Angelou*

Every human being has hundreds of separate people living under his skin. The talent of a writer is his ability to give them their separate names, identities, personalities and have them relate to other characters living with him.
— *Mel Brooks*

Write your first draft with your heart. Rewrite with your head.
— *Mike Rich*

Tomorrow may be hell, but today was a good writing day, and on the good writing days nothing else matters.
— *Neil Gaiman*

I think it's bad to talk about one's present work, for it spoils something at the root of the creative act. It discharges the tension.
— *Norman Mailer*

Serious writers write, inspired or not. Over time they discover that routine is a better friend than inspiration.
— *Ralph Keyes*

The writer is an explorer. Every step is an advance into a new land.
— *Ralph Waldo Emerson*

Your intuition knows what to write, so get out of the way.
— *Ray Bradbury*

Just write every day of your life. Read intensely. Then see what happens.
— *Ray Bradbury*

If you go too far in fantasy and break the string of logic, and become nonsensical, someone will surely remind you of your dereliction ... Pound for pound, fantasy makes a tougher opponent for the creative person.
— *Richard Matheson*

A writer has to force himself to work. He has to make his own hours and if he doesn't go to his desk at all there is nobody to scold him.
— *Roald Dahl*

I know that if I have been working on one paragraph and I have written it three times, it goes in the bin. Unless it comes straight out, it is wrong, it is awkward, it does not fit.
— *Robert Rankin*

The most authentic endings are the ones which are already revolving towards another beginning.
— *Sam Shepard*

You never have to change anything you got up in the middle of the night to write.
— *Saul Bellow*

There are moments in the field when you can't believe what's flowing through you and coming out on the page.
— *Sebastien Junger*

When asked, "How do you write?" I invariably answer, "One word at a time", and the answer is invariably dismissed. But that is all it is.
— *Stephen King*

I try to create sympathy for my characters, then turn the monsters loose.
— *Stephen King*

The scariest moment is always just before you start.
— *Stephen King*

Write. Start writing today. Start writing right now. Don't write it right, just write it — and then make it right later. Give yourself the mental freedom to enjoy the process, because the process of writing is a long one. Be wary of "writing rules" and advice. Do it your way.
— *Tara Moss*

Being an author is having angels whisper in your ear — and devils, too.
— *Terri Guillemets*

I'm not a writer. Ernest Hemingway was a writer. I just have a vivid imagination and type ninety WPM.
— *Tiffany Madison*

I do not over-intellectualize the production process. I try to keep it simple: Tell the damned story.
— *Tom Clancy*

Inspiration always arrives unannounced.
— *Vanna Bonta*

Among the many problems which beset the novelist, not the least weighty is the choice of the moment at which to begin his novel.
— *Vita Sackville-West*

The first thing you have to know about writing is that it is something you must do every day. There are two reasons for this rule: Getting the work done and connecting with your unconscious mind.
— *Walter Mosley*

Always carry a notebook. And I mean always. The short-term memory only retains information for three minutes; unless it is committed to paper you can lose an idea for ever.
— *Will Self*

It is better to write a bad first draft than to write no first draft at all.
— *Will Shetterly*

I only write when I am inspired. Fortunately I am inspired at nine o'clock every morning.
— *William Faulkner*

Read! You'll absorb it. Then write. If it's good, you'll find out. If it's not, throw it out of the window.
— *William Faulkner*

Get it down. Take chances. It may be bad, but it's the only way you can do anything really good.
— *William Faulkner*

It begins with a character, usually, and once he stands up on his feet and begins to move, all I can do is trot along behind him with a paper and pencil trying to keep up long enough to put down what he says and does.
— *William Faulkner*

Protect the time and space in which you write. Keep everybody away from it, even the people who are most important to you.
— *Zadie Smith*

THE PRACTICE OF OUTSTANDING WRITING

James Blish told me I had the worst case of "said bookism"; that is, using every word except "said" to indicate dialogue. He told me to limit the verbs to "said", "replied", "asked", and "answered" and only when absolutely necessary.

— Anne McCaffrey

Do not hoard what seems good for a later place in the book, or for another book; give it, give it all, give it now.

— Annie Dillard

To write well, express yourself like the common people, but think like a wise man.

— Aristotle

The simpler you say it, the more eloquent it is.

— August Wilson

Good things, when short, are twice as good.

— Baltasar Gracian

Slang is a language that rolls up its sleeves, spits on its hands and goes to work.
— *Carl Sandburg*

If the word doesn't exist, invent it; but first be sure it doesn't exist.
— *Charles Baudelaire*

Our admiration of fine writing will always be in proportion to its real difficulty and its apparent ease.
— *Charles Caleb Colton*

Make 'em laugh; make 'em cry; make 'em wait.
— *Charles Reade*

An idea for a story can be anything. The sky is not the limit, the limit is beyond it.
— *Chrys Fey*

Verbose is not a synonym for literary.
— *Constance Hale*

A sentence can offer a moment of quiet, it can crackle with energy or it can just lie there, listless and uninteresting. What makes the difference? The verb.
— *Constance Hale*

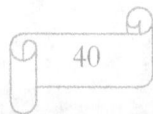

Writers get ideas all day every day. The FedEx guy delivers a package from Sears and the writer is thinking how it could actually be a ticking time bomb.
— *Dan Alatorre*

When one is writing a novel in the first person, one must be that person.
— *Daphne du Maurier*

Pithy sentences are like sharp nails driving truth into our memory.
— *Diderot*

You only learn to be a better writer by actually writing.
— *Doris Lessing*

There are no laws for the novel. There never have been, nor can there ever be.
— *Doris Lessing*

Good writing is supposed to evoke sensation in the reader—not the fact that it is raining, but the feeling of being rained upon.
— *E L Doctorow*

If it sounds like writing, I rewrite it. Or, if proper usage gets in the way, it may have to go. I can't allow what we learned in English composition to disrupt the sound and rhythm of the narrative.
— *Elmore Leonard*

I try to leave out the parts that people skip.
— *Elmore Leonard*

Do not write so that you can be understood, write so that you cannot be misunderstood.
— *Epictetus*

Be careful that you write accurately rather than much.
— *Erasmus*

Easy writing makes hard reading.
— *Ernest Hemingway*

As a writer, you should not judge, you should understand.
— *Ernest Hemingway*

I like to listen. I have learned a great deal from listening carefully. Most people never listen.
— *Ernest Hemingway*

Prose is architecture, not interior decoration.
— *Ernest Hemingway*

When writing a novel a writer should create living people; people not characters. A character is a caricature.
— *Ernest Hemingway*

The good parts of a book may be only something a writer is lucky enough to overhear or it may be the wreck of his whole damn life and one is as good as the other.
— *Ernest Hemingway*

My aim is to put down on paper what I see and what I feel in the best and simplest way.
— *Ernest Hemingway*

Parenthetical remarks (however relevant) are unnecessary.
— *Frank L Visco*

It is my ambition to say in ten sentences what others say in a whole book.
— *Friedrich Nietzsche*

A novelist can do anything he wants so long as he makes people believe in it.
— *Gabriel Garcia Marquez*

The best way to become a successful writer is to read good writing, remember it, and then forget where you remember it from.

— *Gene Fowler*

The finest language is mostly made up of simple unimposing words.

— *George Eliot*

Never use a metaphor, simile, or other figure of speech which you are used to seeing in print.

— *George Orwell*

Never use a long word where a short one will do.

— *George Orwell*

I think myself I ought to be shot for writing such nonsense … But it's unquestionably good escapist literature, and I think I should rather like it if I were sitting in an air-raid shelter or recovering from flu.

— *Georgette Heyer*

The great advantage of being a writer is that you can spy on people. You're there, listening to every word, but part of you is observing. Everything is useful to a writer, you see — every scrap.

— *Graham Greene*

Whatever sentence will bear to be read twice, we may be sure was thought twice.
> — *Henry David Thoreau*

Not that the story need be long, but it will take a long while to make it short.
> — *Henry David Thoreau*

Write while the heat is in you … The writer who postpones the recording of his thoughts uses an iron which has cooled to burn a hole with.
> — *Henry David Thoreau*

To produce a mighty book, you must choose a mighty theme.
> — *Herman Melville*

One gains universal applause who mingles the useful with the agreeable, at once delighting and instructing the reader.
> — *Horace*

You will have written exceptionally well if, by skilful arrangement of your words, you have made an ordinary one seem original.
> — *Horace*

I made up my mind long ago to follow one cardinal rule in all my writing — to be "clear". I have given up all thought of writing poetically or symbolically or experimentally, or in any of the other modes that might (if I were good enough) get me a Pulitzer prize. I would write merely clearly and in this way establish a warm relationship between myself and my readers, and the professional critics — Well, they can do whatever they wish.

— *Isaac Asimov*

There's a rule of writing: if everything is funny, nothing is funny; if everything is sad, nothing is sad. You want that contrast.

— *J Michael Straczynski*

To practice — write each and every day if possible — then try to attend professional writers' conferences where you can learn your craft, get to know fellow writers, and meet editors and agents.

— *James Dashner*

I've put in so many enigmas and puzzles that it will keep the professors busy for centuries arguing over what I meant, and that's the only way of insuring one's immortality.

— *James Joyce*

One tends to write beyond what's needed.
> — *James Schuyler*

The thing that makes vivid writing is when the reader is in the body of the story, the body of the character. Things smell like something; there's weather, there's texture, there's light.
> — *Janet Fitch*

You learn to write by writing, and by reading and thinking about how writers have created their characters and invented their stories. If you are not a reader, don't even think about being a writer.
> — *Jean M Auel*

First, have something to say. Second, say it. Third, stop when you have said it. Fourth, give it a good title.
> — *John Shaw Billings*

I have found it helps to pick out one real person I know and write to that one person.
> — *John Steinbeck*

If you are using dialogue — say it aloud as you write it. Only then will it have the sound of speech.
> — *John Steinbeck*

There's a great power in words, if you don't hitch too many of them together.
— *Josh Billings*

Writers don't forget the past; they turn it into raw material.
— *Joyce Rachelle*

You always get more respect when you don't have a happy ending.
— *Julia Quinn*

Style means the right word. The rest matters little.
— *Jules Renard*

People are much more complicated in real life, but my characters are as subtle and nuanced as I can make them. But if you say my characters are too black and white, you've missed the point. Villains are meant to be black-hearted in popular novels. If you say I have a grey-hearted villain, then I've failed.
— *Ken Follett*

Every sentence must do one of two things — reveal character or advance the action.
— *Kurt Vonnegut*

Give your readers as much information as possible as soon as possible.
— *Kurt Vonnegut*

Give the reader at least one character he or she can root for.
— *Kurt Vonnegut*

Be a sadist. No matter how sweet and innocent your leading characters, make awful things happen to them — in order that the reader may see what they are made of.
— *Kurt Vonnegut*

Write. Rewrite. When not writing or rewriting, read. I know of no shortcuts.
— *Larry L King*

I think ... the most brilliant thing about being a writer is that if you don't like the way the world is, you can create your own.
— *Maegan Cook*

Write quickly and you will never write well; write well, and you will soon write quickly.
— *Marcus Fabius Quintilianus*

Prune what is turgid, elevate what is commonplace, arrange what is disorderly, introduce rhythm where the language is harsh, modify where it is too absolute.

— *Marcus Fabius Quintilianus*

Whatever is hidden behind the curtain must be revealed at last, and it must be at one and the same time completely unexpected and inevitable.

— *Margaret Atwood*

Any writer overwhelmingly honest about pleasing himself is almost sure to please others.

— *Marianne Moore*

The difference between the almost right word and the right word is really a large matter — it's the difference between the lightning bug and the lightning.

— *Mark Twain*

To get the right word in the right place is a rare achievement. To condense the diffused light of a page of thought into the luminous flash of a single sentence, is worthy to rank as a prize composition just by itself ... Anybody can have ideas — the difficulty is to express them without squandering a quire of paper on an idea that ought to be reduced to one glittering paragraph.

— *Mark Twain*

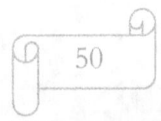

Substitute "damn" every time you're inclined to write "very"; your editor will delete it and the writing will be just as it should be.
— *Mark Twain*

As to the adjective, when in doubt, strike it out.
— *Mark Twain*

You must write for children in the same way as you do for adults, only better.
— *Maxim Gorky*

Easy reading is damn hard writing. But if it's right, it's easy. It's the other way round, too. If it's slovenly written, then it's hard to read. It doesn't give the reader what the careful writer can give the reader.
— *Maya Angelou*

Write the kind of story you would like to read.
— *Meg Cabot*

If you are not writing something you like, no one else will like it either.
— *Meg Cabot*

From Ernest Hemingway's stories, I learned to listen within my stories for what went unsaid by my characters.
— *Nadine Gordimer*

Metaphors have a way of holding the most truth in the least space.
— *Orson Scott Card*

Everybody walks past a thousand story ideas every day. The good writers are the ones who see five or six of them. Most people don't see any.
— *Orson Scott Card*

Dialogue has only two purposes: (1) to enhance the character, and (2) to further the plot.
— *Othello Bach*

Words are the raw material of our craft. The greater your vocabulary the more effective your writing.
— *P D James*

Your job as a writer is to find storylines, narrative structures, and characters to show the things that you believe rather than saying them or telling them.
— *Philipp Meyer*

When I write, I try to think back to what I was afraid of or what was scary to me, and try to put those feelings into books.
— *R L Stine*

Confident writers have the courage to speak plainly; to let their thoughts shine rather than their vocabulary.
— *Ralph Keyes*

Let the world burn through you. Throw the prism light, white hot, on paper.
— *Ray Bradbury*

Remember: Plot is no more than footprints left in the snow after your characters have run by on their way to incredible destinations.
— *Ray Bradbury*

The secret of good writing is to say an old thing in a new way or to say a new thing in an old way.
— *Richard Harding Davis*

A writer must learn to deepen characters, trim writing, intensify scenes.
— *Richard North Patterson*

In the best fiction, the language itself can become almost invisible.
— *Robert Morgan*

It is with words as with sunbeams. The more they are condensed, the deeper they burn.
— *Robert Southey*

It looks like the writer is telling you a story. What the writer is actually doing, however, is using words to evoke a series of micro-memories from your own experience that inmix, join, and connect in your mind in an order the writer controls, so that, in effect, you have a sustained memory of something that never happened to you.
— *Samuel R Delany*

Every great and original writer, in proportion as he is great or original, must himself create the taste by which he is to be relished.
— *Samuel Taylor Coleridge*

Write about what makes you different.
— *Sandra Cisneros*

Someone told me that each equation I include in the book would halve the sales.
— *Stephen Hawking*

When a good writer is having fun, the audience is almost always having fun too.
— *Stephen King*

A little talent is a good thing to have if you want to be a writer. But the only real requirement is the ability to remember every scar.
— *Stephen King*

If you don't have time to read, you don't have the time (or the tools) to write. Simple as that.
— *Stephen King*

The road to hell is paved with adverbs.
— *Stephen King*

Description begins in the writer's imagination, but should finish in the reader's.
— *Stephen King*

Any word you have to hunt for in a thesaurus is the wrong word. There are no exceptions to this rule.
— *Stephen King*

People are always saying you should write what you know, but I love to write what I don't know.
— *Teresa Medeiros*

Let grammar, punctuation, and spelling into your life! Even the most energetic and wonderful mess has to be turned into sentences.
— *Terry Pratchett*

The most valuable of all talents is that of never using two words when one will do.
— *Thomas Jefferson*

The difference between reality and fiction? Fiction has to make sense.
— *Tom Clancy*

The one thing emphasized in any creative writing course is "Write what you know", and that automatically drives a wooden stake through the heart of imagination. If they really understood the mysterious process of creating fiction, they would say, "You can write about anything you can imagine."
— *Tom Robbins*

You can't blame a writer for what the characters say.
— *Truman Capote*

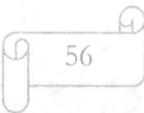

The idea that it is necessary to go to a university in order to become a successful writer ... is one of those phantasies that surround authorship.

— *Vera Brittain*

A woman must have money and a room of her own if she is to write fiction.

— *Virginia Woolf*

It's not a writer's business to hold opinions.

— *W B Yeats*

To write simply is as difficult as to be good.

— *W Somerset Maugham*

If you can tell stories, create characters, devise incidents, and have sincerity and passion, it doesn't matter a damn how you write.

— *W Somerset Maugham*

Hard writing makes easy reading.

— *Wallace Stegner*

Read, read, read. Read everything — trash, classics, good and bad, and see how they do it.

— *William Faulkner*

Verbs are the action words of the language and the most important. Turn to any passage on any page of a successful novel and notice the high percentage of verbs.
— *William Sloan*

Vigorous writing is concise. A sentence should contain no unnecessary words, a paragraph no unnecessary sentence, for the same reason that a drawing should have no unnecessary lines and a machine no unnecessary parts.
— *William Strunk*

THE PROOFREADING, EDITING, AND REVISION STAGES

An editor is someone who separates the wheat from the chaff and then prints the chaff.
                    — *Adlai Stevenson*

You become a good writer just as you become a good joiner: by planing down your sentences.
                    — *Anatole France*

Almost all good writing begins with terrible first efforts. You need to start somewhere.
                    — *Anne Lamott*

Revision is one of the true pleasures of writing.
                    — *Bernard Malamud*

Writers' bedtimes vary, but few have been spared the shock of a copy editor's early wake-up call.
                    — *Bill Walsh*

Put down everything that comes into your head and then you're a writer. But an author is one who can judge his own stuff's worth, without pity, and destroy most of it.
— *Colette*

I can't write five words but that I change seven.
— *Dorothy Parker*

Rereading reveals rubbish and redundance.
— *Duane Alan Hahn*

Rewriting ripens what you've written.
— *Duane Alan Hahn*

An editor is a person who knows more about writing than writers do but who has escaped the terrible desire to write.
— *E B White*

The best writing is rewriting.
— *E B White*

What is easy to read has been difficult to write. The labour of writing and rewriting, correcting and recorrecting, is the due exacted by every good book from its author, even if he knows from the beginning exactly what he wants to say.
— *G. M. Trevelyan*

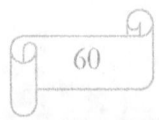

No passion in the world is equal to the passion to alter someone else's draft.
— *H.G. Wells*

I'm not a very good writer, but I'm an excellent rewriter.
— *James A Michener*

There are two typos of people in this world: Those who can edit and those who can't.
— *Jarod Kintz*

Half my life is an act of revision.
— *John Irving*

No matter how wonderful a sentence is, if it doesn't add new, useful information it should be removed.
— *Kurt Vonnegut*

There is no great writing, only great rewriting.
— *Louis Brandeis*

Books aren't written — they're rewritten. Including your own. It is one of the hardest things to accept, especially after the seventh rewrite hasn't quite done it.
— *Michael Crichton*

You can fix anything but a blank page.
— *Nora Roberts*

I was working on the proof of one of my poems all the morning, and took out a comma. In the afternoon I put it back again.
— *Oscar Wilde*

I enjoy rewriting much more than I enjoy first drafts. First drafts are really hard. Rewriting you've at least got something to work with.
— *Robin Hobb*

When both my editors say, "This is really bad, you need to change this", I ignore that at my peril.
— *Robin Hobb*

Read over your composition, and where ever you meet with a passage which you think is particularly fine, strike it out.
— *Samuel Johnson*

My first draft is usually how I meant it, but my second and third drafts are how I want to be understood.
— *Selena Haskins*

Write with the door closed, rewrite with the door open.
— *Stephen King*

When your story is ready for rewrite, cut it to the bone. Get rid of every ounce of excess fat. This is going to hurt; revising a story down to the bare essentials is always a little like murdering children, but it must be done.
— *Stephen King*

Some editors are failed writers, but so are most writers.
— *T S Eliot*

There are two kinds of editors, those who correct your copy and those who say it's wonderful.
— *Theodore H White*

Everyone needs an editor.
— *Tim Foote*

I cannot think of anybody who doesn't need an editor, even though some people claim they don't.
— *Toni Morrison*

I believe more in the scissors than I do the pencil.
— *Truman Capote*

Proofread carefully to see if you any words out.
— *William Safire*

THE PERSISTENT WRITER

I tell writers to keep reading, reading, reading. Read widely and deeply. And I tell them not to give up even after getting rejection letters. And only write what you love.
— *Anita Diamant*

The secret to being a writer is that you have to write. It's not enough to think about writing or to study literature or to plan a future life as a writer. You really have to lock yourself away, alone, and get to work.
— *Augusten Burroughs*

A one-hundred-thousand-word novel might take a year or several years, and then you just come to "The End" one day. But it takes hundreds of days to get to "The End". As a writer, you have to put in those hundreds of days.
— *Bob Mayer*

If you write one story, it may be bad; if you write a hundred, you have the odds in your favour.
— *Edgar Rice Burroughs*

Like stones, words are laborious and unforgiving, and the fitting of them together, like the fitting of stones, demands great patience and strength of purpose and particular skill.
— *Edmund Morrison*

It's none of their business that you have to learn how to write. Let them think you were born that way.
— *Ernest Hemingway*

It's not a career for anyone who needs security. It's a career for gamblers. It's a career of ups and downs.
— *George R R Martin*

In my view a writer is a writer not because she writes well and easily, because she has amazing talent, because everything she does is golden. In my view a writer is a writer because even when there is no hope, even when nothing you do shows any signs of promise, you keep writing anyway.
— *Junot Diaz*

The secret of becoming a writer is to write, write and keep on writing.
— *Ken MacLeod*

I could write an entertaining novel about rejection slips, but I fear it would be overly long.
— *Louise Brown*

Everybody writes a book too many.
— *Mordecai Richler*

First forget inspiration. Habit is more dependable. Habit will sustain you whether you're inspired or not. Habit will help you finish and polish your stories. Inspiration won't. Habit is persistence in practice.
— *Octavia E Butler*

You don't start out writing good stuff. You start out writing crap and thinking it's good stuff, and then gradually you get better at it.
That's why I say one of the most valuable traits is persistence.
— *Octavia E Butler*

The writer's secret is not inspiration — for it is never clear where it comes from — it is his stubbornness, his patience.
— *Orhan Pamuk*

A professional writer is an amateur who didn't quit.
— *Richard Bach*

It took me fifteen years to discover I had no talent for writing, but I couldn't give it up because by that time I was too famous.
— *Robert Benchley*

Very little about being a writer is signing an autograph. It's sitting in a room and writing. Getting it out.
— *Robin Hobb*

The harder you work as a writer, the better you get at it. It's like anything else. It's a muscle you have to exercise.
— *Ron White*

I took my writing seriously, and it seemed to pay off.
— *Samuel R Delany*

A man may write at any time, if he will set himself doggedly to it.
— *Samuel Johnson*

Volume depends precisely on the writer's having been able to sit in a room every day, year after year, alone.
— *Susan Sonntag*

The writer's duty is to keep on writing.
— *William Styron*

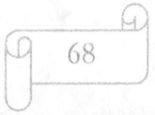

THE PROLIFIC WRITER

I have always tried to write in a simple way, using down-to-earth and not abstract words.

— Georges Simenon (500 books)

I guess I'm prolific because I have a simple and straightforward style.

— Isaac Asimov (500 books)

If my doctor told me I had only six minutes to live, I wouldn't brood. I'd type a little faster.

— Isaac Asimov

Quantity produces quality. If you only write a few things, you're doomed.

— Ray Bradbury (27 novels, 600 short stories)

These are quotes from writers on being prolific. Some other prolific writers whose quotes are included in this book, but not in this section, include:

Agatha Christie (66 mystery novels, 6 romances, 14 short story collections; 2 billion books sold worldwide).

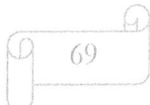

Alexander Dumas (100,000 pages of stories, serials, novels and nonfiction).

G K Chesterton (80 books, 200 short stories, 4000 essays, hundreds of poems).

Nora Roberts (200+ novels, also writes as J D Robb; romance and fantasy genres).

Ruth Rendell (70+ novels, including as Barbara Vine; mostly mysteries).

Stephen King (50+ novels; horror genre).

THE PASSION OF WRITING

Don't just write a strong female protagonist. Be one.
— *A D Posey*

Words can be like X-rays if you use them properly —
they'll go through anything. You read and you're pierced.
— *Aldous Huxley*

The secret of genius is to carry the spirit of the child into
old age, which means never losing your enthusiasm.
— *Aldous Huxley*

A bad book is as much a labour to write as a good one; it
comes as sincerely from the author's soul.
— *Aldous Huxley*

Infatuated, half through conceit, half through love of my
art, I achieve the impossible working as no one else ever
works.
— *Alexandre Dumas*

If you do not breathe through writing, if you do not cry out in writing, or sing in writing, then don't write, because our culture has no use for it.
— *Anaïs Nin*

I can shake off everything as I write; my sorrows disappear, my courage is reborn.
— *Anne Frank*

I loved words. I love to sing them and speak them and even now, I must admit, I have fallen into the joy of writing them.
— *Anne Rice*

Every writer knows fear and discouragement. Just write. The world is crying for new writing. It is crying for fresh and original voices and new characters and new stories. If you won't write the classics of tomorrow, well, we will not have any.
— *Anne Rice*

You're a reader as well as a writer, so write what you'd want to read.
— *Cassandra Clare*

Write what you know. Write what you want to know more about. Write what you're afraid to write about.
— *Cec Murphy*

Write with the complete palette of emotions.
— *Cindy Lambert*

A writer falls in love with an idea and gets carried away.
— *Doris Lessing*

I wish I could write as mysterious as a cat.
— *Edgar Allan Poe*

Not knowing when the dawn will come, I open every door.
— *Emily Dickinson*

A writer never has a vacation. For a writer, life consists either of writing or thinking about writing.
— *Eugene Ionesco*

Follow your most intense obsessions mercilessly.
— *Franz Kafka*

When I am writing best, I really am lost in my world. I lose track of the outside world. I have a difficult time balancing between my real world and the artificial world.
— *George R R Martin*

The writer must believe that what he is doing is the most important thing in the world. And he must hold to this illusion even when he knows it is not true.
— *John Steinbeck*

You have to write the book that wants to be written. And if the book will be too difficult for grown-ups, then you write it for children.
— *Madeline L'Engle*

A good writer reveals beauty in the mundane and truth in tragedy. Words are a tool; a currency of the mind, and the best writers weave passages into our hearts that our bones remember.
— *Maria Reeves*

Dreams are illustrations ... from the book your soul is writing about you.
— *Marsha Norman*

The idea is to write it so that people hear it and it slides through the brain and goes straight to the heart.
— *Maya Angelou*

You can't use up creativity. The more you use, the more you have.
— *Maya Angelou*

Writing is the indelible fingerprint of my soul on paper.
— *Michelle L Buckley*

Write what disturbs you, what you fear, what you have not been willing to speak about. Be willing to be split open.
— *Natalie Goldberg*

Good fiction creates its own reality.
— *Nora Roberts*

You know you've read a good book when you turn the last page and feel a little as if you have lost a friend.
— *Paul Sweeney*

Tears are words that need to be written.
— *Paulo Coelho*

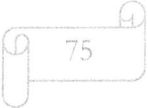

Writing *with voice* is writing into which someone has breathed. It has that fluency, rhythm, and liveliness that exist naturally in the speech of most people when they are enjoying a conversation. Writing with *real voice* has the power to make you pay attention and understand — the words go deep.

         — *Peter Elbow*

You must stay drunk on writing so reality cannot destroy you.

         — *Ray Bradbury*

The artist must bow to the monster of his own imagination.

         — *Richard Wright*

No tears in the writer, no tears in the reader. No surprise in the writer, no surprise in the reader.

         — *Robert Frost*

Words are, of course, the most powerful drug used by mankind.

         — *Rudyard Kipling*

What one writer can make in the solitude of one room is something no power can easily destroy.

         — *Salman Rushdie*

When once the itch of literature comes over a man, nothing can cure it but the scratching of a pen.
— *Samuel Lover*

You cannot hope to sweep someone else away by the force of your writing until it has been done to you.
— *Stephen King*

Writing is magic, as much the water of life as any other creative art. The water is free. So drink. Drink and be filled up.
— *Stephen King*

Books are a uniquely portable magic.
— *Stephen King*

Let me live, love and say it well in good sentences.
— *Sylvia Plath*

Some authors write with a grave ink, of a dramatic pen dipped into their dark souls.
— *Terri Guillemets*

The story is not in the plot but in the telling.
— *Ursula K Le Guin*

A writer is a person who cares what words mean, what they say, how they say it. Writers know words are their way towards truth and freedom, and so they use them with care, with thought, with fear, with delight. By using words well they strengthen their souls. Storytellers and poets spend their lives learning that skill and art of using words well. And their words make the souls of their readers stronger, brighter, deeper.
— *Ursula K Le Guin*

The real story is not the plot, but how the characters unfold by it.
— *Vanna Bonta*

Every secret of a writer's soul, every experience of his life, every quality of his mind, is written large in his works.
— *Virginia Woolf*

Fill your paper with the breathings of your heart.
— *William Wordsworth*

THE PRIVACY OF WRITING

I don't know much about creative writing programs. But they're not telling the truth if they don't teach, one, that writing is hard work, and, two, that you have to give up a great deal of life, your personal life, to be a writer.
— *Doris Lessing*

Writing is utter solitude, the descent into the cold abyss of oneself.
— *Franz Kafka*

Writing is a solitary occupation. Family, friends and society are the natural enemies of the writer. He must be alone, uninterrupted, and slightly savage if he is to sustain and complete an undertaking.
— *Jessamyn West*

In utter loneliness a writer tries to explain the inexplicable.
— *John Steinbeck*

If you are a writer you locate yourself behind a wall of silence and no matter what you are doing, driving a car or walking or doing housework you can still be writing, because you have that space.
— *Joyce Carol Oates*

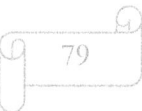

I am a recluse at present & do nothing but write & read & read & write.
— *Katherine Mansfield*

I think to be a writer you have to enjoy being alone.
— *Markus Zusak*

Writers don't have lifestyles. They sit in little rooms and write.
— *Norman Mailer*

I never want to see anyone, and I never want to go anywhere or do anything. I just want to write.
— *P G Wodehouse*

Writing is a solitary experience. I'm extremely superstitious. If I talk about the book or name the title out loud before finishing, I feel the energy I need to write will be drained. It's so intimate, I can't even share it with my wife.
— *Paulo Coelho*

The writer is a mysterious figure, wandering lonely as a cloud, fired by inspiration, or perhaps a cocktail or two.
— *Sara Sheridan*

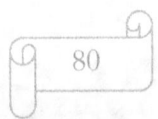

The writer is either a practising recluse or a delinquent, guilt-ridden one; or both. Usually both.
— *Susan Sonntag*

A writer needs a life of introspection.
— *Tony Robbins*

THE PERFECTIONIST

Perfection is achieved, not when there is nothing more to add, but when there is nothing left to take away.
— *Antoine de Saint-Exupery*

A great writer creates a world of his own and his readers are proud to live in it. A lesser writer may entice them in for a moment, but soon he will watch them filing out.
— *Cyril Connolly*

I am learning that perfection isn't what matters. In fact, it's the very thing that can destroy you if you let it.
— *Emily Giffin*

The really great writers are people like Emily Bronte who sit in a room and write out of their limited experience and unlimited imagination.
— *James A Michener*

The proper words in the proper places are the true definition of style.
— *Jonathan Swift*

More can be learnt from Miss Austen about the nature of the novel than from almost any other writer.
— *Walter Allen*

THE PERNICIOUS

The relationship between critic and writer is similar to the one between the pigeon and the statue.
— *Ashwin Sanghi*

Give me six lines written by the most honourable of men, and I will find an excuse in them to hang him.
— *Cardinal Richelieu*

There are books of which the backs and covers are by far the best parts.
— *Charles Dickins*

I think that if a third of all the novelists and maybe two-thirds of all the poets now writing dropped dead suddenly, the loss to literature would not be great.
— *Charles Osborne*

Many suffer from the incurable disease of writing, and it becomes chronic in their sick minds.
— *Decimus Junius Juvenalis*

If you want to get rich from writing, write the sort of thing that's read by persons who move their lips when they're reading to themselves.
— *Don Marquis*

Do you realize that all great literature is all about what a bummer it is to be a human being? Isn't it such a relief to have somebody say that?
— *Kurt Vonnegut*

When someone is mean to me, I just make them a victim in my next book.
— *Mary Higgins Clark*

Authors are easy to get on with — if you're fond of children.
— *Michael Joseph*

The reciprocal civility of authors is one of the most risible scenes in the farce of life.
— *Samuel Johnson*

People who say you'll never amount to much as a writer (or even those exhibiting indifference) are speaking from gross ignorance. They are comparing your stumbling, incomplete draft – seen or unseen – and their anecdotal knowledge of you as a person to their favourite writer's best-selling novel. Unfair in the extreme.

— *Scott Nicol*

Being an author is being in charge of your own personal insane asylum.

— *Terri Guillemets*

THE PAIN OF WRITING

I have always had more dread of a pen, a bottle of ink, and a sheet of paper than of a sword or pistol.
— *Alexandre Dumas*

I suffer from the disease of writing books and being ashamed of them when they are finished.
— *Baron de Montesquieu*

Writing is really very easy. Tap a vein and bleed onto the page. Everything else is just technical.
— *Derrick Jensen*

Writing a novel is a terrible experience, during which the hair often falls out and the teeth decay. I'm always irritated by people who imply that writing fiction is an escape from reality. It is a plunge into reality and it's very shocking to the system.
— *Flannery O'Connor*

The writer operates at a peculiar crossroads where time and space and eternity somehow meet. His problem is to find that location.
— *Flannery O'Connor*

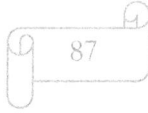

A non-writing writer is a monster courting insanity.
— *Franz Kafka*

I think we ought to read only the kind of books that wound and stab us.
— *Franz Kafka*

I write differently from what I speak, I speak differently from what I think, I think differently from the way I ought to think, and so it all proceeds into deepest darkness.
— *Franz Kafka*

Writing is easy: all you do is sit staring at a blank piece of paper until drops of blood form on your head.
— *Gene Fowler*

Writing a book is a horrible, exhausting struggle, like a long bout with some painful illness. One would never undertake such a thing if one were not driven on by some demon whom one can neither resist nor understand.
— *George Orwell*

Writing is not a profession but a vocation of unhappiness.
— *Georges Simenon*

Writing is a delicious agony.
— *Gwendolyn Brooks*

I would advise anyone who aspires to a writing career that before developing his talent he would be wise to develop a thick hide.
— *Harper Lee*

The actual writers I know are experts in neurotic self-torture. Every page of writing is the result of a thousand tiny decisions and desperate acts of will.
— *Helen Garner*

Rejection slips, or form letters, however tactfully phrased, are lacerations of the soul, if not quite inventions of the devil — but there is no way around them.
— *Isaac Asimov*

Any writer, I suppose, feels that the world into which he was born is nothing less than a conspiracy against the cultivation of his talent.
— *James Baldwin*

When I'm not writing I feel an awareness that something's missing. If I go a long time, it becomes worse.
— *Jennifer Egan*

Writing is so difficult that I often feel that writers, having had their hell on earth, will escape all punishment thereafter.
— *Jessamyn West*

If there is a special Hell for writers it would be in the forced contemplation of their own works.
— *John Dos Passos*

It's part of a writer's profession, as it's part of a spy's profession, to prey on the community to which he's attached, to take away information — often in secret — and to translate that into intelligence for his masters, whether it's his readership or his spy masters. And I think that both professions are perhaps rather lonely.
— *John Le Carre*

The writer must be universal in sympathy and an outcast by nature; only then can he see clearly.
— *Julian Barnes*

You cannot be a good writer of serious fiction if you are not depressed.
— *Kurt Vonnegut*

If I don't write to empty my mind, I go mad.
— *Lord Byron*

Writers are the exorcists of their own demons.
— *Mario Vargas Llosa*

The writing career is not a romantic one. The writer's life may be colourful, but his work itself is rather drab.
— *Mary Roberts Reinhart*

There is no greater agony than bearing an untold story inside you.
— *Maya Angelou*

Writing can wreck your body. You sit there on the chair hour after hour and sweat your guts out to get a few words.
— *Norman Mailer*

Writing is pretty crummy on the nerves.
— *Paul Theroux*

The road to hell is paved with works-in-progress.
— *Philip Roth*

It's hell writing and it's hell not writing. The only tolerable state is having just written.
— *Robert Hass*

I discovered that rejections are not altogether a bad thing. They teach a writer to rely on his own judgment and to say in his heart of hearts, "To hell with you."
— *Saul Bellow*

If it was easy, everyone would do it rather than going around telling you their ideas and saying how they could be a writer if they had the time.
— *Stanisław Lem*

Nothing stinks like a pile of unpublished writing.
— *Sylvia Plath*

I think it's good for a writer to think he's dying; he works harder.
— *Tennessee Williams*

Writing is a dreadful labour, yet not so dreadful as idleness.
— *Thomas Carlyle*

THE PLEASURE OF WRITING

When a writer talks about his work, he's talking about a love affair.
— *Alfred Kazin*

I have never known any distress that an hour's reading did not relieve.
— *Charles De Montesquieu*

The love of reading enables a man to exchange the wearisome hours of life which come to everyone for hours of delight.
— *Charles De Montesquieu*

Next to doing things that deserve to be written, nothing gets a man more credit, or gives him more pleasure than to write things that deserve to be read.
— *Lord Chesterfield*

I love telling stories. I love the intimacy between the writer and reader.
— *David Walliams*

I hate writing, I love having written.
— *Dorothy Parker*

You can find magic wherever you look. Sit back and relax, all you need is a book.
— *Dr Seuss*

The more you write, the more potential there is for growth.
— *Elizabeth Lowell*

The desire to write grows with writing.
— *Erasmus*

Once writing has become your major vice and greatest pleasure, only death can stop it.
— *Ernest Hemingway*

There is no friend as loyal as a book.
— *Ernest Hemingway*

I do not like to write — I like to have written.
— *Gloria Steinem*

Do not read, as children do, to amuse yourself, or like the ambitious, for the purpose of instruction. No, read in order to live.

— Gustave Flaubert

Writing is its own reward.

— Henry Miller

Wherever I am, if I've got a book with me, I have a place I can go and be happy.

— J K Rowling

I love writing. I love the swirl and swing of words as they tangle with human emotions.

— James A Michener

Real luxury is time and opportunity to read for pleasure.

— Jane Brody

It's a dream come true to get paid for what I love to write.

— K A Mitchell

For one who reads, there is no limit to the number of lives that may be lived.

— Louis L'Amour

Reading is a discount ticket to everywhere.
— *Mary Schmich*

People talk about the pain of writing, but very few people talk about the pleasure and satisfaction.
— *Paul Theroux*

Writing is the most fun you can have by yourself.
— *Terry Pratchett*

THE PHILOSOPHICAL

Writing a book is like telling a joke and having to wait two years to know whether or not it was funny.
— *Alain de Botton*

Those who write clearly have readers; those who write obscurely have commentators.
— *Albert Camus*

It is the function of art to renew our perception. What we are familiar with we cease to see. The writer shakes up the familiar scene, and, as if by magic, we see a new meaning in it.
— *Anaïs Nin*

Asking a writer what he thinks about critics is like asking a lamp post how it feels about dogs.
— *Ann Landers*

Literature is all, or mostly, about sex.
— *Anthony Burgess*

You don't have to say everything to say something.
— *Beth Moore*

I really believe that a writer is someone who has trained their mind to misbehave.
— *Brad Thor*

Science fiction is no more written for scientists than ghost stories are written for ghosts.
— *Brian Aldiss*

Reading is a means of thinking with another person's mind; it forces you to stretch your own.
— *Charles Scribner*

Better to write for yourself and have no public, than to write for the public and have no self.
— *Cyril Connolly*

Read a lot. Write a lot. Have fun.
— *Daniel Pinkwater*

It is better to read a little and ponder a lot than to read a lot and ponder a little.
— *Denis Parsons Burkitt*

A good story is always more dazzling than a broken piece of truth.
— *Diane Setterfield*

Be who you are and say what you feel, because those who mind don't matter, and those who matter don't mind.
— *Dr Seuss*

Sometimes the questions are complicated and the answers are simple.
— *Dr Seuss*

You're never too old, too wacky, too wild, to pick up a book and read to a child.
— *Dr Seuss*

Writing is an act of faith, not a trick of grammar.
— *E B White*

Writing is both mask and unveiling.
— *E B White*

True originality consists not in a new manner but in a new vision.
— *Edith Wharton*

Beneath the rule of men entirely great, the pen is mightier than the sword.
— *Edward Bulwer-Lytton*

The writer, when he is also an artist, is someone who admits what others don't dare reveal.
— *Elia Kazan*

Creativity requires the courage to let go of certainties.
— *Erich Fromm*

A writer of fiction is really … a congenital liar who invents from his own knowledge or that of other men.
— *Ernest Hemingway*

All good books are alike in that they are truer than if they had really happened and after you are finished reading one you will feel that all that happened to you and afterwards it all belongs to you; the good and the bad, the ecstasy, the remorse and sorrow, the people and the places and how the weather was. If you can get so that you can give that to people, then you are a writer.
— *Ernest Hemingway*

Writers aren't people, exactly. Or, if they're any good, they're a whole lot of people trying so hard to be one person.
— *F Scott Fitzgerald*

An original writer is not one who imitates nobody, but one whom nobody can imitate.
— *François-René de Chateaubriand*

The gift of words is the gift of deception and illusion.
— *Frank Herbert*

Many a book is like a key to unknown chambers within the castle of one's own self.
— *Franz Kafka*

A good writer possesses not only his own spirit but also the spirit of his friends.
— *Friedrich Nietzsche*

A good novel tells us the truth about its hero; but a bad novel tells us the truth about its author.
— *G K Chesterton*

You could compile the worst book in the world entirely out of selected passages from the best writers in the world.
— *G K Chesterton*

Literature — creative literature — unconcerned with sex, is inconceivable.
— *Gertrude Stein*

Writing is a dog's life, but the only life worth living.
— *Gustave Flaubert*

There are no dull subjects. There are only dull writers.
— *H L Mencken*

One can be absolutely truthful and sincere even though admittedly the most outrageous liar. Fiction and invention are of the very fabric of life.
— *Henry Miller*

It is the writer who might catch the imagination of young people, and plant a seed that will flower and come to fruition.
— *Isaac Asimov*

Fiction writing is great. You can make up almost anything.
— *Ivana Trump*

Life is too short for reading inferior books.
— *James Bryce*

Mistakes are the portals of discovery.
— *James Joyce*

Being a writer means taking the leap from listening to saying, "Listen to me".
— *Jhumpa Lahiri*

The act of reading is a partnership. The author builds a house, but the reader makes it a home.
— *Jodi Picoult*

In nearly all good fiction, the basic - all but inescapable - plot form is this: A central character wants something, goes after it despite opposition (perhaps including his own doubts), and so arrives at a win, lose, or draw.
— *John Gardner*

I know that books seem like the ultimate thing that's made by one person, but that's not true. Every reading of a book is a collaboration between the reader and the writer who are making the story up together.
—*John Green*

I guess there are never enough books.
— *John Steinbeck*

Reading is to the mind what exercise is to the body.
— *Joseph Addison*

To live a creative life we must first lose the fear of being wrong.
> — *Joseph Chilton Pearce*

Women with clean houses do not have finished books.
> — *Joy Held*

Writing is an occupation in which you have to keep proving your talent to those who have none.
> — *Jules Renard*

To be alive and to be a "writer" is enough.
> — *Katherine Mansfield*

We have to continually be jumping off cliffs and developing our wings on the way down.
> — *Kurt Vonnegut*

It was very lucky for me as a writer that I studied the physical sciences rather than English. I wrote for my own amusement. There was no kindly English professor to tell me for my own good how awful my writing really was. And there was no professor with the power to order me what to read, either.
> — *Kurt Vonnegut*

Being a writer is like having homework every night for the rest of your life.
— *Lawrence Kasdan*

Fantasy is hardly an escape from reality. It's a way of understanding it.
— *Lloyd Alexander*

As a writer, the best mind set is to be unafraid.
— *Malcolm Gladwell*

A home without books is a body without soul.
— *Marcus Tullius Cicero*

You need three things to become a successful novelist: talent, luck and discipline.
— *Michael Chabon*

To be a writer you need to drink in the world around you so it's always there in your head.
— *Michael Morpurgo*

The first chapter sells the book; the last chapter sells the next book.
— *Mickey Spillane*

Fundamentally, all writing is about the same thing; it's about dying, about the brief flicker of time we have here, and the frustration that it creates.
— *Mordecai Richler*

Fiction is about stuff that's screwed up.
— *Nancy Kress*

Stories may well be lies, but they are good lies that say true things, and which can sometimes pay the rent.
— *Neil Gaiman*

There is no such thing as a moral or an immoral book. Books are well written, or badly written.
— *Oscar Wilde*

A writer is someone who has taught his mind to misbehave.
— *Oscar Wilde*

If one cannot enjoy reading a book over and over again, there is no use in reading it at all.
— *Oscar Wilde*

A writer is, after all, only half his book. The other half is the reader and from the reader the writer learns.
— *P L Travers*

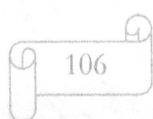

After nourishment, shelter and companionship, stories are the thing we need most in the world.
— *Philip Pullman*

Writing is, in the end, that oddest of anomalies: an intimate letter to a stranger.
— *Pico Lyer*

If we encounter a man of rare intellect, we should ask him what books he reads.
— *Ralph Waldo Emerson*

You don't have to burn books to destroy a culture. Just get people to stop reading them.
— *Ray Bradbury*

I don't care if a reader hates one of my stories, just as long as he finishes the book.
— *Roald Dahl*

Who said time machines haven't been built yet? They already exist. They're called books.
— *Robert Benchley*

Authors like cats because they are such quiet, lovable, wise creatures, and cats like authors for the same reasons.
— *Robertson Davies*

The faults of great authors are generally excellences carried to an excess.
— *Samuel Taylor Coleridge*

Fiction is the truth inside the lie.
— *Stephen King*

We live under continual threat of two equally fearful, but seemingly opposed destinies: unremitting banality and inconceivable terror. It is fantasy, served out in large rations by the popular arts, which allows most people to cope with these twin spectres.
— *Susan Sonntag*

Writing is writing, and stories are stories. Perhaps the only true genres are fiction and nonfiction. And even there, who can be sure?
— *Tanith Lee*

If science fiction is the mythology of modern technology, then its myth is tragic.
— *Ursula K Le Guin*

When you're a writer, you hear your internal critic, and that's really hard to get over. And then sometimes you hear critiques from classmates and stuff. But when a book comes out, it's just hundreds of opinions and you have to learn to separate out the ones you want to listen to or figure out how many you want to listen to.
— *Veronica Roth*

A novelist is, like all mortals, more fully at home on the surface of the present than in the ooze of the past.
— *Vladimir Nabokov*

Literature is strewn with the wreckage of those who have minded beyond reason the opinion of others.
— *Virginia Woolf*

If you do not tell the truth about yourself you cannot tell it about other people.
— *Virginia Woolf*

Writing is like sex. First you do it for love, then you do it for your friends, and then you do it for money.
— *Virginia Woolf*

One great use of words is to hide our thoughts.
— *Voltaire*

Some books are undeservedly forgotten; none are undeservedly remembered.
— *W H Auden*

Only a mediocre writer is always at his best.
— *W Somerset Maugham*

Writers, like teeth, are divided into incisors and grinders.
— *Walter Bagehot*

Clear writers, like clear fountains, do not seem so deep as they are; the turbid look the most profound.
— *Walter Savage Landor*

A writer needs three things, experience, observation, and imagination, any two of which, at times any one of which, can supply the lack of the others.
— *William Faulkner*

I divide all readers into two classes: those who read to remember and those who read to forget.
— *William Lyon Phelps*

THE PUNS, PARODIES AND OTHER FUNNY STUFF

A committed writer sentences himself to death.
> — *unknown*

A synonym is a word you use when you can't spell the word you first thought of.
> — *Burt Bacharach*

Writers should be read, but neither seen nor heard.
> — *Daphne du Maurier*

I love deadlines. I love the whooshing noise they make as they go by.
> — *Douglas Adams*

Writing is a socially acceptable form of schizophrenia.
> — *E L Doctorow*

Everywhere I go I'm asked if I think the university stifles writers. My opinion is that they don't stifle enough of them. There's many a bestseller that could have been prevented by a good teacher.
> — *Flannery O'Connor*

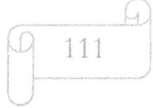
111

Our principal writers have nearly all been fortunate in escaping regular education.
— *Hugh MacDiarmid*

How do you know when a novel is finished? When the deadline is approaching.
— *Ian Rankin*

Writing is like getting married. One should never commit oneself until one is amazed at one's luck.
— *Iris Murdoch*

When I was a little boy they called me a liar but now that I am grown up they call me a writer.
— *Isaac Bashevis Singer*

Any fool can write a novel but it takes real genius to sell it.
— *J G Ballard*

You can't wait for inspiration. You have to go after it with a club.
— *Jack London*

Writing is the only profession where no one considers you ridiculous if you earn no money.
— *Jules Renard*

Writing is a way of talking without being interrupted.
— *Jules Renard*

A writer is someone who can make a riddle out of an answer.
— *Karl Kraus*

Writing is show business for shy people.
— *Lee Child*

Writing is the hardest way of earning a living, with the possible exception of wrestling alligators.
— *Olin Miller*

I love talking about nothing. It is the only thing I know anything about.
— *Oscar Wilde*

I never travel without my diary. One should always have something sensational to read in the train.
— *Oscar Wilde*

I love being a writer. What I can't stand is the paperwork.
— *Peter De Vries*

So, please, oh please, we beg, we pray, go throw your TV set away, and in its place you can install, a lovely bookcase on the wall.
— *Roald Dahl*

The freelance writer is a man who is paid per piece or per word or perhaps.
— *Robert Benchley*

The beautiful part of writing is that you don't have to get it right the first time, unlike, say, a brain surgeon.
— *Robert Cormier*

I am the literary equivalent of a Big Mac and Fries.
— *Stephen King*

There are three rules for writing a novel. Unfortunately, no one knows what they are.
— *W Somerset Maugham*

If you steal from one author, it's plagiarism; if you steal from many, it's research.
— *Wilson Mizner*

THE POTENT QUOTES

You don't write because you want to say something, you write because you have something to say.
— *F Scott Fitzgerald*

If there's a book you really want to read, but it hasn't been written yet, then you must write it.
— *Toni Morrison*

You fail only if you stop writing.
— *Ray Bradbury*

Amateurs sit and wait for inspiration, the rest of us just get up and go to work.
— *Stephen King*

If I waited for perfection, I would never write a word.
— *Margaret Atwood*

This is how you do it: you sit down at the keyboard and you put one word after another until it's done. It's that easy, and that hard.
— *Neil Gaiman*

Don't tell me the moon is shining; show me the glint of light on broken glass.
— *Anton Chekhov*

Write what should not be forgotten.
— *Isabel Allende*

The most important thing is to read as much as you can, like I did.
— *J K Rowling*

Read a thousand books, and your words will flow like a river.
— *Lisa See*

I've learned that people will forget what you said, people will forget what you did, but people will never forget how you made them feel.
— *Maya Angelou*

What is written without effort is in general read without pleasure.
— *Samuel Johnson*

It is perfectly okay to write garbage — as long as you edit brilliantly.
> — *C J Cherryh*

The first draft of anything is shit.
> — *Ernest Hemingway*

If it is possible to cut a word out, always cut it out.
> — *George Orwell*

You can always edit a bad page. You can't edit a blank page.
> — *Jodi Picoult*

If you want to be a writer, you must do two things above all others: read a lot and write a lot. There's no way around these two things that I'm aware of, no shortcut.
> — *Stephen King*

I don't think there is enough respect in general for the time it takes to write consistently good fiction. Too many people think they will master writing overnight, or that they are as good as they will ever be.
> — *Tananarive Due*

Discipline allows magic. To be a writer is to be the very best of assassins. You do not sit down and write every day to force the Muse to show up. You get into the habit of writing every day so that when she shows up, you have the maximum chance of catching her, bashing her on the head, and squeezing every last drop out of that bitch.

— *Lili St Crow*

Write the stories that excite you, stories you can't wait to share with the world because they're just so amazing … And if you must obsess over something, obsess over stuff like tension and pacing and creating believable characters. You know, the shit that matters. There are no writing police. This is your story, no one else's. Tell it like you want to.

— *Rachel Aaron*

You don't find time to write. You make time.

— *Nora Roberts*

Write in a way that scares you a little.

— *Holley Gerth*

Through my characters — not through some plot — I can make readers laugh, or cringe, or cry.

— *Judith McNaught*

In order to write the book you want to write, in the end you have to become the person you need to become to write that book.
— *Junot Diaz*

We are all apprentices in a craft where no one ever becomes a master.
— *Ernest Hemingway*

At night, when the objective world has slunk back into its cavern and left dreamers to their own, there come inspirations and capabilities impossible at any less magical and quiet hour. No one knows whether or not he is a writer unless he has tried writing at night.
— *H P Lovecraft*

There is nothing to writing. All you do is sit down at a typewriter and bleed.
— *Ernest Hemingway*

It is a writer's greatest pleasure to hear that someone was kept up until the unholy hours of the morning reading one of his books.
— *Brandon Sanderson*

Writing is the only thing that, when I do it, I don't feel I should be doing something else.
— *Gloria Steinem*

Reading and weeping opens the door to one's heart, but writing and weeping opens the window to one's soul.
— *M K Simmons*

I just love writing. It's magical, it's somewhere else to go, it's somewhere much more dreadful, somewhere much more exciting.
— *Tanith Lee*

Which of us has not felt that the character we are reading in the printed page is more real than the person standing beside us?
— *Cornelia Funke*

The profession of book-writing makes horse racing seem like a solid, stable business.
— *John Steinbeck*

I am, really, a great writer; my only difficulty is in finding great readers.
— *Frank Harris*

This sentence has five words. Here are five more words. Five-word sentences are fine. But several together become monotonous. Listen to what is happening. The writing is getting boring. The sound of it drones. It's like a stuck record. The ear demands some variety. Now listen. I vary the sentence length, and I create music. Music. The writing sings. It has a pleasant rhythm, a lilt, a harmony. I use short sentences. And I use sentences of medium length. And sometimes, when I am certain the reader is rested, I will engage him with a sentence of considerable length, a sentence that burns with energy and builds with all the impetus of a crescendo, the roll of the drums, the crash of the cymbals — sounds that say listen to this, it is important.

— *Gary Provost (from 100 Ways to Improve Your Writing)*

NOTES, AND YOUR OWN QUOTES

QUOTES ON WRITING

QUOTES ON WRITING

QUOTES ON WRITING

QUOTES ON WRITING

QUOTES ON WRITING

QUOTES ON WRITING